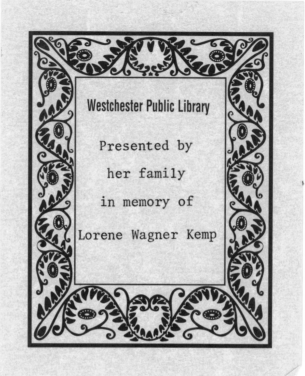

For Joanna

First published in 1991 by
Blackie and Son Limited
7 Leicester Place, London WC2H 7BP

Copyright © Prue Theobalds 1991

British Library Cataloguing in Publication Data
Old MacDonald had a farm.
    1.   Children's songs in English
    I.   Theobalds, Prue *1936-*
782.42

    ISBN 0-216-93092-8
    ISBN 0-216-93093-6 pbk

First American edition published in 1991 by
Peter Bedrick Books
2112 Broadway, New York, NY 10023

Library of Congress Cataloging-in-Publication Data
Theobalds, Prue.
    Old MacDonald had a farm / Prue Theobalds. – 1st American ed.
    Summary: The inhabitants of Old MacDonald's farm are described,
verse by verse, as the illustrations follow them through the four
seasons.
    ISBN 0-87226-452-1
    1.   Folk-songs, English – United States – Texts.   [1.   Folk songs,
American.]   I.   Title.
    PZ8.3.T2601   1991
    782.42162′13′00268 – dc20   90-14417
                                    CIP
                                      AC

Printed in Hong Kong by Wing King Tong Co Ltd
10 9 8 7 6 5 4 3 2 1

Old MacDonald Had a Farm

The Traditional Nursery Song

Illustrated by
Prue Theobalds

Blackie
London

Bedrick/Blackie
New York

Old MacDonald had a farm, E–I–E–I–O!
And on that farm he had some sheep, E–I–E–I–O!
With a baa, baa here and a baa, baa there,
Here a baa, there a baa, everywhere a baa, baa,
Old MacDonald had a farm, E–I–E–I–O!

Old MacDonald had a farm, E–I–E–I–O!
And on that farm he had some dogs, E–I–E–I–O!
With a woof, woof here and a woof, woof there,
Here a woof, there a woof, everywhere a woof, woof,
Old MacDonald had a farm, E–I–E–I–O!

Old MacDonald had a farm,
  E–I–E–I–O!
And on that farm he had a horse,
  E–I–E–I–O!
With a neigh, neigh here
And a neigh, neigh there,
Here a neigh, there a neigh,
Everywhere a neigh, neigh,
Old MacDonald had a farm,
  E–I–E–I–O!

Old MacDonald had a farm, E–I–E–I–O!
And on that farm he had some geese, E–I–E–I–O!
With a honk, honk here and a honk, honk there,
Here a honk, there a honk, everywhere a honk, honk,
Old MacDonald had a farm E–I–E–I–O!

Old MacDonald had a farm, E–I–E–I–O!
And on that farm he had some cows, E–I–E–I–O!
With a moo, moo here and a moo, moo there,
Here a moo, there a moo, everywhere a moo, moo,
Old MacDonald had a farm, E–I–E–I–O!

Old MacDonald had a farm, E–I–E–I–O!
And on that farm he had some chickens, E–I–E–I–O!
With a cluck, cluck here and a cluck, cluck there,
Here a cluck, there a cluck, everywhere a cluck, cluck,
Old MacDonald had a farm, E–I–E–I–O!

Old MacDonald had a farm, E–I–E–I–O!
And on that farm he had some ducks, E–I–E–I–O!
With a quack, quack here and a quack, quack there,
Here a quack, there a quack, everywhere a quack, quack,
Old MacDonald had a farm, E–I–E–I–O!

Old MacDonald had a farm, E–I–E–I–O!
And on that farm he had some goats, E–I–E–I–O!
With a meh, meh here and a meh, meh there,
Here a meh, there a meh, everywhere a meh, meh,
Old MacDonald had a farm, E–I–E–I–O!

Old MacDonald had a farm, E–I–E–I–O!
And on that farm he had some pigs, E–I–E–I–O!
With an oink, oink here and an oink, oink there,
Here an oink, there an oink, everywhere an oink, oink,
Old MacDonald had a farm, E–I–E–I–O!

Old MacDonald had a farm, E–I–E–I–O!
And on that farm he had some cats, E–I–E–I–O!
With a miaow, miaow here and a miaow, miaow there,
Here a miaow, there a miaow,
  everywhere a miaow, miaow,
Old MacDonald had a farm, E–I–E–I–O!

Old MacDonald had a farm, E–I–E–I–O!
And on that farm he had some turkeys, E–I–E–I–O!
With a gobble, gobble here and a gobble, gobble there,
Here a gobble, there a gobble, everywhere a gobble, gobble,
Old MacDonald had a farm, E–I–E–I–O!

Old MacDonald had a farm, E–I–E–I–O!
And on that farm he had a donkey, E–I–E–I–O!

With a hee-haw here and a hee-haw there,
Here a hee, there a haw, everywhere a hee-haw,
Old MacDonald had a farm, E–I–E–I–O!